TWINS!

TWINS!

by ELAINE SCOTT

photographs by

MARGARET MILLER

ATHENEUM BOOKS FOR YOUNG READERS

Atheneum Books for Young Readers
An imprint of Simon & Schuster Children's Publishing Division
1230 Avenue of the Americas
New York, New York 10020

Book design by Nina Barnett
The text of this book is set in Triplex.

First Edition
Printed in Singapore
10 9 8 7 6 5 4 3 2 1

Library of Congress Cataloging-in-Publication Data
Scott, Elaine.
Twins! / by Elaine Scott ; photographs by Margaret Miller.—1st ed.
p. cm.
ISBN 0-689-80347-8
1. Twins—Juvenile literature. I. Miller, Margaret, date. II. Title.
HQ777.35.S36 1998
306.875—dc21
97-5049

For all the wonderful children in this book:

Ryan and Griffin
Ashton and Tarquinn
Paul, Isaac, and Claire
Evelyn, Eleanor, and Emily
J. D., Sarah, and Dylan
Amos and Charlie
Alice and Hattie
Aamir and Malik

Most mommies give birth to their children one baby at a time. But sometimes a mommy will give birth to two babies instead of just one—TWINS!

When twins arrive in a family there is
twice as much fun,
twice as much **work,**
and twice as much **love**
to go around.

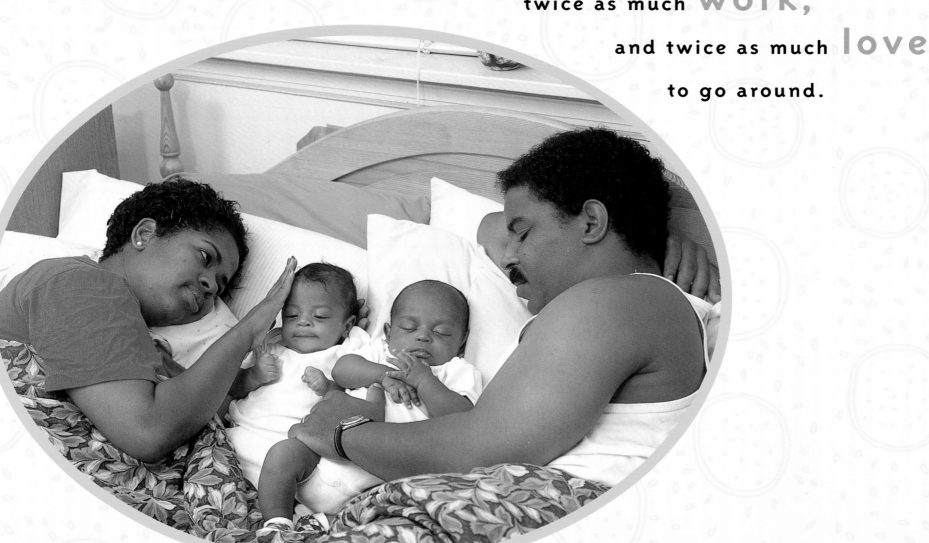

Isaac and Paul are **IDENTICAL TWINS.**
They have the same color hair and the same color eyes.
Identical twins are always two boys or two girls.

Most people have a hard time telling identical
twins apart, but the people who know them well
can always tell the difference.

Evelyn and Eleanor are identical twins too.
They often like to play the same games
and eat the same food.

If they were your friends,
how could you tell them apart?

Sarah and J. D. are **FRATERNAL TWINS.**

So are Griffin and Ryan.

It is easier to tell these children apart
because Sarah and Ryan are girls, and J. D. and Griffin are boys.

But Amos and Charlie and Hattie and Alice are fraternal twins too. Fraternal twins can be two boys or two girls or one of each. Fraternal twins are as alike— or unalike—as other brothers and sisters.

What is different about each of these children? What is the same?

Some twins like to **dress the same.** Evelyn and Eleanor's daddy watches as his dressed-alike girls build a block tower.

Other twins choose **different clothing.** "My favorite color is red," says Isaac. "I'm different. My favorite color is blue," adds Paul.

When twins arrive in a home there is plenty of extra work.

It takes **both Mommy and Daddy**

to feed Tarquinn and Ashton.

Two lively girls make getting dressed a real adventure!

Emily loves being a big sister.
She often **helps** her mother **take care** of Eleanor and Evelyn.

However, twins get a lot of attention. That can be hard for their sisters or brothers. Emily says,

"Sometimes I wish people would notice me, too."

Isaac and Paul's big sister, Claire, says, "I like being their big sister, but my little brothers can be a pain—especially when I'm trying to practice."

"But sometimes **we play** the piano **together**," she adds.

Twins grow up side by side.

They learn to play together. And they learn how to share.

Like all good friends, twins often play the same game.

Aamir and

Malik

enjoy

playing

with

different toys.

Learning to share is as hard for twins as it is for anyone else. Charlie and Amos both want to ride the stick horse, and they **fight** over it.

Is it hard for you to share your favorite toy?

Twins must share other things too. Evelyn and Eleanor share their sister, Emily.

Twins even share their friends. "Dylan is my best friend," says Sarah. "He's my best friend too," adds J. D.

Eleanor
and Evelyn

share

their

daddy

with each

other,

while Sarah
and J. D.
share
reading
time
with
Mommy.

Like all twins, Malik and Aamir will always share their birthday.

Their family celebrates this special day with two choruses of "Happy Birthday" and two different cakes.

Some friends bring the **same present** for each child. Others bring different gifts.

Would you want the same birthday present as your brother or sister, or a different one?

Time alone with Mommy or Daddy is always special for twins.

When their brother or sister is away, there are romps on the bed with Mommy . . .

. . . and cuddles with Daddy. Everyone needs times that don't have to be shared.

Being
a twin
means
having
someone
just
your age
to
share
secrets,

kisses, and a good case of the giggles!

Fraternal
or identical,
being a
twin is fun—
and special.
But all people
are special.

Whether you are a twin or not, you are unique.
There is no one else in the world exactly like you, and that is
the most special thing of all!

Parent's Note

How to Use This Book with Your Child

"When I was growing up, being a twin had its freaky side," said one young woman, a twin herself and now mother to six-year-old twins of her own. "Now there are so many of us that people are gaining a better understanding of what it means to be a twin and to have twins." It is my hope that this book will broaden that understanding for today's families. **It is not written just for families of multiples. It is intended for use with all children** who, sooner or later, will meet and befriend sets of twins in their preschool or neighborhood adventures.

In the United States forty years ago, the arrival of a set of twins was a remarkable occurrence. Now it is much more commonplace. On a recent trip to the zoo, another mother of twins stated, "It was like Twin City—there were zillions of us there!" Thanks to

changes in reproductive techniques and women delaying motherhood until their mid-thirties, multiple births are booming, and for today's children **being a twin or relating to twins is a familiar experience.**

However, curiosity and questions seem to go with the territory that surrounds twins, and adults are not the only ones who ask. Other children are naturally curious and spontaneous in their reaction to twins—especially identicals. One mother reported that a preschooler spotted her identical twin sons in the mall, stared hard at them, and exclaimed, "Look! Those boys have the same face!" Indignant, one boy responded, "I have my own face!"

If your child happens to be friendly with a set of identical twins, it helps if you as the parent could say something like, "Paul and Isaac may look alike to you, but they look different to their mommy and daddy." Not only is this a statement of fact, it reassures the "singleton" child as well, since all **children need to know that they are unique** and hold their own irreplaceable spot in their parents' hearts.

Fraternal twins are often inadvertently put in the spot of defending their "twinship." **"You're twins? You don't look alike!"** is a frequent comment from adults and children. It is usually well-meaning, but can sound almost accusatory. A good way to respond to statements similar to this is a simple, "Amos and Charlie don't look alike because they are two different little boys."

I have referred to the children in this book by their given names, never as "the so-and-so twins." It seemed important to me, to them, and to their parents to emphasize their individuality. And the truth is, fraternal twins are no more alike than any other siblings—they simply share a birth date. In fact all twins, whether fraternal or identical, **deserve to be treated as the different individuals they are.**

Although most preschool children will not ask how twins are created, their older siblings

may have questions. I have not taken up space in the text of this book to explain the process, since there are already many excellent books for young children that deal with conception and birth, most notably Joanna Cole and Margaret Miller's *How You Were Born,* published by Mulberry Paperback Books in 1994. Building on the information

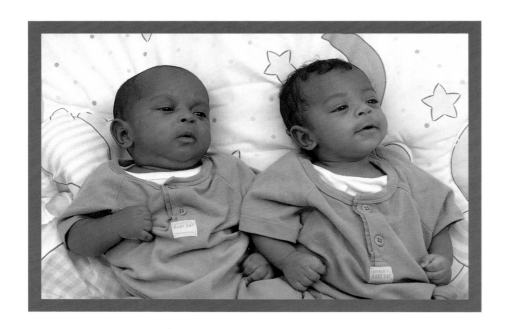

contained in texts like that one, a parent can explain the differences between fraternal and identical twins in the simplest possible terms.

If this book generates questions about how twins are conceived, **fraternal twinning might be explained as** simply as this: "Most mothers produce one egg cell each month. If it is fertilized by a father's sperm cell, one baby will begin to grow inside the mother. Occasionally, some mothers produce two—or even more—egg cells in one month. If those egg cells are fertilized by the father's sperm cells, then two or more babies will begin to grow inside the mother. The babies are born at the same time. But because each baby begins with a different egg cell and a different sperm cell, these children are really no more alike than other brothers and sisters who arrive one at a time."

Or, **to explain how identical twins are conceived you could use language** similar to this: "Identical twins occur when one egg cell and one sperm cell grow and divide and begin to make one baby. Then something special happens. Those cells divide themselves in half. Each half continues to multiply, and two identical babies begin to grow inside their mother. Because they begin with the same egg cell and the same sperm cell, these babies will be identical twins." Watch your child's reaction as you explain these "facts of life." **You may be telling much more than the child wanted to know!**

Parents of twins with whom I talked as I prepared this manuscript were eager to emphasize the **joy their children bring them and the individuality of each child,** though they also mentioned the frustration of not having enough time to give plenty of attention to everyone in the family! Most understood the public's curiosity, but **grew weary of questions that were intrusive.** "Are they twins?" topped the list of "most-asked" questions, but it is not the question that bothers parents most. Questions like "Which one is the smart one, the creative one, the lazy one?" are not welcome, since twins, like the rest of the population, share equally in the distribution of character traits—good and bad. **Also unwelcome are comments** such as "You poor thing," **"Double trouble!"** or "Just wait

till they start walking!" As one mother of three-year-old twins and a five-year-old single-ton child said, **"It's a blessing, not a curse.** It's a special relationship that few people ever get to experience. It's a wild life, but I wouldn't trade it for anything."

This book is intended as a celebration of each child's individuality, as well as their "twinship." **It is designed to be interactive,** posing questions for discussion on many dif-

ferent topics. Of course, the questions are only suggestions. You or your children may think of others as you read through the text together. Being a twin and/or relating to twins is rapidly becoming a commonplace experience. In the United States, fraternal twins are born once in 80 births, and identicals arrive once in every 250 births—**doubling the work, love, and laughter in the homes they grace.**